3036

Wolfgang Amadeus
MOZART

Music for One Piano/Four Hands

DISC A

DISC B

MMO 3036A

Music Minus One

Banjo

___	MMO 4401	Bluegrass Banjo
___	MMO 4402	How to Play 5-String Banjo, v. I
___	MMO 4403	How to Play 5-String Banjo, v. II

Bassoon

___	MMO 4601	Solos For The Bassoon
___	MMO 4602	Masterpieces for Woodwind Quintet
___	MMO 4603	The Joy of Woodwind Quintets
___	MMO 4604	STRAVINSKY L'Histoire du Soldat
___	MMO 4605	BEETHOVEN Quintet in E-flat major, op. 16
___	MMO 4606	MOZART Quintet in E-flat major, KV452
___	**MMO 4607**	**VIVALDI Concerto E minor, F.VIII/6 (RV484); Concerto C major, F.VIII/17 (RV472) (2CD)**

Clarinet in A

___	**MMO 3207**	**MOZART Quintet A major, KV581 (Remastered - 2CD)**
___	**MMO 3230**	**BRAHMS Quintet B minor, op. 115 (Remastered - 2CD)**
___	**MMO 3238**	**MOZART Clarinet Concerto A major, KV622 (2CD)**

Clarinet in B-flat

___	MMO 3202	WEBER Clarinet Concerto No. 1 F minor, op. 73; STAMITZ Clarinet Concerto No. 3 B-flat
___	MMO 3203	SPOHR Clarinet Concerto No. 1 C minor, op. 26
___	MMO 3204	WEBER Clarinet Concertino, op. 26, J109; BEETHOVEN Trio No. 4, op. 11
___	MMO 3205	First Chair Clarinet Solos: Orchestral Excerpts
___	MMO 3206	Art of the Solo Clarinet: Orchestral Excerpts
___	**MMO 3207**	**MOZART Quintet A major, KV581 (Remastered - 2CD)**
___	MMO 3208	BRAHMS Sonata F minor, op.120, no.1; Sonata E-flat major, op.120, no.-2
___	MMO 3209	WEBER Grand Duo; WAGNER Adagio
___	MMO 3210	SCHUMANN Phantasiestücke, op. 73; 3 Romanzen, op. 94
___	MMO 3211	Easy Clarinet Solos, v. I - Student Level
___	MMO 3212	Easy Clarinet Solos, v. II - Student Level
___	MMO 3213	Easy Jazz Duets for 2 Clarinets & Rhythm Section
___	MMO 3214	Visions: Ron Odrich (2CD)
___	MMO 3217	STRAVINSKY L'Histoire du Soldat
___	MMO 3218	Jazz Standards w/Rhythm Section (2 CD)
___	MMO 3219	Jazz Standards with Strings (2 CD)
___	MMO 3221	Beginning Clarinet Solos, v. I (J. Bunke)
___	MMO 3222	Beginning Clarinet Solos, v. II (H. Wright)
___	MMO 3223	Intermediate Clarinet Solos, v. I (S. Drucker)
___	MMO 3224	Intermediate Clarinet Solos, v. II (J. Bunke)
___	MMO 3225	Advanced Clarinet Solos, v. I (S. Drucker)
___	MMO 3226	Advanced Clarinet Solos, v. II (H. Wright)
___	MMO 3227	Intermediate Clarinet Solos, v. III (S. Drucker)
___	MMO 3228	Advanced Clarinet Solos, v. III (S. Drucker)
___	MMO 3229	Advanced Clarinet Solos, v. IV (H. Wright)
___	**MMO 3230**	**BRAHMS Clarinet Quintet B min, op. 115 (Remastered - 2CD)**
___	MMO 3231	Teacher's Partner: Basic Clarinet Studies
___	MMO 3232	Jewels for Woodwind Quintet
___	MMO 3233	Masterpieces for Woodwind Quintet
___	MMO 3234	From Dixie to Swing
___	MMO 3235	BEETHOVEN Quintet E-flat major, op. 16
___	MMO 3236	MOZART Quintet E-flat major, KV452
___	MMO 3237	Stompin' & Struttin' the New Swing
___	**MMO 3238**	**MOZART Concerto A major, KV622 (NEW RECORDING - 2CD)**
___	**MMO 3239**	**Traditional Jazz Series: Chicago-Style Jam Session (2CD)**
___	**MMO 3240**	**Virtuoso Clarinet: Baermann, op. 63 (4CD)**
___	**MMO 3241**	**Art of Clarinet: Baermann, op. 64 (4CD)**
___	MMO 3242	Popular Concert Favorites with Orchestra
___	MMO 3243	Band Aids: Concert Band Favorites w/Orch
___	MMO 3244	World Favorites: 41 Easy Selections
___	MMO 3245	Classic Themes: 27 Easy Songs
___	**MMO 3246**	**HAJDU Jewish Rhapsody for Clarinet and Orchestra**
___	**MMO 3247**	**20 Rhythm Backgrnds to Standards (Expnd./Remastered 2CD)**

___	MMO 3829	When Jazz Was Young: Bob Wilber
___	MMO 4104	For Saxes Only: Bob Wilber
___	MMO 4205	Bluesaxe: Blues for Saxophone
___	MMO 4209	Play Lead a Sax Section: The Bob Wilber All-Stars
___	MMO 4210	Days of Wine & Roses

Double Bass

___	**MMO 2047**	**2+2=5: A Study Odd Times**
___	MMO 4301	Beginning to Intermediate Contest Solos
___	MMO 4302	Intermediate to Advanced Contest Solos
___	MMO 4303	For Bassists Only (Ken Smith)
___	MMO 4304	The Beat Goes On
___	MMO 4305	From Dixie to Swing
___	MMO 4306	STRAVINSKY L'Histoire du Soldat
___	MMO 4307	SCHUBERT Quintet A major, op. 114, 'Trout'
___	**MMO 4308**	**BOTTESINI Concerto B minor; Grande Allegro di Concerto (2CD)**

Drums

___	**MMO 2048**	**2+2=5: A Study Odd Times**
___	MMO 5001	Modern Jazz Drumming (2 CD)
___	MMO 5002	For Drummers Only: Jazz Band Music
___	MMO 5003	Wipe-Out
___	MMO 5004	Sit-with Jim Chapin
___	MMO 5005	Drum Star Jazz Combos
___	MMO 5006	Drum Pad Stick Skin: Jazz play-alongs
___	MMO 5007	Jump, Jive and Wail: 6 Swing Bands
___	MMO 5009	Classical Percussion (2 CD)
___	MMO 5010	Eight Men Search of a Drummer
___	MMO 5011	From Dixie to Swing
___	MMO 5013	Open Session: Greg Burrows Quint. (2 CD)
___	MMO 5014	STRAVINSKY L'Histoire du Soldat

Flute

___	MMO 3159	HAYDN Trios, v. I: F major (HobXV:17), D major (HobXV:16), and G major (HobXV:15)
___	MMO 3301	MOZART Concerto No. 1 in G, KV313(KV285d)
___	MMO 3302	J.S. BACH Suite No. 2 in B minor, BWV1067
___	MMO 3303	BOCCHERINI Concerto in D; VIVALDI Concerto No. 2 G min 'La Notte'; MOZART Andante
___	MMO 3304	HAYDN Divertimento D major; VIVALDI Concerto D major, op. 10 No. 3; FREDERICK THE GREAT Concerto C major
___	**MMO 3305**	**VIVALDI Flute Concerto F major (RV433); TELEMANN Flute Concerto D maj; LECLAIR Flute Concerto C major (2CD)**
___	MMO 3306	J.S. BACH Brandenburg Concerto No. 2 F major; HAYDN Flute Concerto No. 9 D minor
___	MMO 3307	J.S. BACH 'Triple' Concerto A minor, BWV1044; VIVALDI Concerto D minor, RV236
___	MMO 3308	MOZART Quartet F major, KV370 (KV368b); STAMITZ Quartet F major, op. 8, no. 3
___	MMO 3309	HAYDN 4 'London' Trios HobIV:1-4
___	MMO 3310	J.S. BACH Brandenburg Concerti Nos. 4 in G (BWV1049) & 5 in D (BWV1050)
___	MMO 3311	MOZART 3 Quartets in D, C and A
___	MMO 3312	TELEMANN Suite A minor; GLUCK 'Orfee' scene; PERGOLESI Concerto in G (2CD) (Avail. 17 Mar)
___	MMO 3313	Flute Song: Easy Familiar Classics w/Orch.
___	MMO 3314	VIVALDI Flute Concerti D major (RV427); F major (RV434); G major (RV438)
___	MMO 3315	VIVALDI Flute Concerti D major (RV429); G major (RV435); A minor (RV440)
___	**MMO 3316**	**Easy Flute Solos: v. 1**
___	**MMO 3317**	**Easy Flute Solos: v. II (Remastered/2CD)**
___	MMO 3318	Easy Jazz Duets: 2 Flutes & Rhythm Section
___	**MMO 3319**	**Flute/Guitar Duets, v.I (Remastered/2CD)**
___	MMO 3321	Beginning Flute Solos, v. I (M. Panitz)
___	MMO 3322	Beginning Flute Solos, v. II (D. Peck)
___	MMO 3323	Intermediate Flute Solos, v. I (J. Baker)

MMO 3324	Intermediate. Flute Solos, v. II (D. Peck)	
MMO 3325	Advanced Flute Solos, v. I (M. Panitz)	
MMO 3326	Advanced Flute Solos, v. II (J. Baker)	
MMO 3327	Intermediate Flute Solos, v. III (D. Peck)	
MMO 3328	Advanced Flute Solos, v. III (M. Panitz)	
MMO 3329	Advanced Flute Solos, v. IV (J. Baker)	
MMO 3330	Beginning Flute Solos, v. III (D. Dwyer)	
MMO 3331	Intermediate Flute Solos, v. IV (D. Dwyer)	
MMO 3332	Advanced Flute Solos, v. V (D. Dwyer)	
MMO 3333	First Chair Solos with Orchestra	
MMO 3334	Teacher's Partner: First Year Flute Studies	
MMO 3335	The Joy of Woodwind Music	
MMO 3336	Jewels for Woodwind Quintet	
MMO 3340	3 Sonatas (Händel & Telemann)	
MMO 3341	3 Sonatas (Telemann, Händel & Marcello)	
MMO 3342	BOLLING Suite for Flute and Jazz Trio	
MMO 3343	HÄNDEL 3 Sonatas; TELEMANN 3 Duet Sonatas (2 CD)	
MMO 3344	J.S. BACH Flute Sonata No. 1 B min, BWV1030/ KUHLAU Two Duets (2 CD)	
MMO 3345	KUHLAU Trio E-flat major; BACH Sonatas E-flat and A maj (2 CD)	
MMO 3346	PEPUSCH Sonata C; TELEMANN Sonata C minor	
MMO 3347	QUANTZ Trio Sonata C minor; BACH Gigue; ABEL Sonata No. 2 F major	
MMO 3348	TELEMANN Concerto No. 1 D major/ CORRETTE Sonata E minor	
MMO 3349	TELEMANN Trio F major, B-flat; HÄNDEL Sonata No. 3 C major	
MMO 3350	HÄNDEL; MARCELLO; TELEMANN Sonatas F major	
MMO 3351	Concert Band Favorites with Orchestra	
MMO 3352	Band Aids: Concert Band Favorites	
MMO 3354	World Favorites: 41 Easy Selections	
MMO 3355	Classic Themes: 27 Easy Songs	
MMO 3356	Renaissance Dances and Fantasias	
MMO 3357	Echoes of Time (2 CD)	
MMO 3358	Eighteenth Century Recorder Music (2 CD)	
MMO 3359	English Consort Music (2 CD)	
MMO 3360	Dances of Three Centuries	
MMO 3361	**MOZART Concerto Flt & Hrp C major K299 (3CD)**	
MMO 3362	**MOZART Concerto No. 2 in D, KV314; QUANTZ Concerto in G (New Recording/2CD)**	
MMO 3363	**HAYDN Three Trios: F (HobXV:17), D (HobXV:16), and G (HobXV:15)**	
MMO 3364	**PIAZZOLLA Histoire du Tango**	
MMO 3370	**VERACINI Four Sonatas**	
MMO 3371	**Romantic Classics for Flute & Piano (2CD)**	

French Horn (in F)

MMO 3501	MOZART Concerto No. 2 Eb K417; No. 3 Eb K447	
MMO 3502	Baroque Brass and Beyond: Quintets	
MMO 3503	Music for Brass Ensemble	
MMO 3504	MOZART 12 Pieces for 2 Horns, KV487	
MMO 3505	BEETHOVEN Quintet in E-flat major, op. 16	
MMO 3506	MOZART Quintet in E-flat major, KV452	
MMO 3511	Beginning French Horn Solos, v. I (M. Jones)	
MMO 3512	Beginning French Horn Solos, v. II (M. Bloom)	
MMO 3513	Intermediate French Horn Solos, v. I (D. Clevenger)	
MMO 3514	Intermediate French Horn Solos, v. II (M. Jones)	
MMO 3515	Advanced French Horn Solos, v. I (M. Bloom)	
MMO 3516	Advanced French Horn Solos, v. II (Clevenger)	
MMO 3517	Intermediate French Horn Solos, v. III (M. Jones)	
MMO 3518	Advanced French Horn Solos, v. III (M. Bloom)	
MMO 3519	Intermediate French Horn Solos, v. IV (D. Clevenger)	
MMO 3520	French Horn Woodwind Music	
MMO 3521	Masterpieces for Woodwind Quintet	
MMO 3522	French Horn Up Front Brass Quintets	
MMO 3523	Horn of Plenty Brass Quintets	
MMO 3524	Band Aids for French Horn: Concert Band Favorites with Orch	

Guitar

MMO 3601	BOCCHERINI Guitar Quintet No. 4 in D	
MMO 3602	GIULIANI Guitar Quintet A major, op. 65	
MMO 3603	Classic Guitar Duets	
MMO 3604	Renaissance & Baroque Guitar Duets	
MMO 3605	Classical & Romantic Guitar Duets	
MMO 3606	**Guitar/Flute Duets, v. I (Remastered/2CD)**	
MMO 3608	Bluegrass Guitar	
MMO 3609	Play the Guitar: The Easy Way to Learn	
MMO 3610	How To Play the Folk Guitar (2CD)	
MMO 3611	Favorite Folks Songs For Guitar	
MMO 3612	For Guitarists Only! Jimmy Raney	
MMO 3613	Ten Duets for Two Guitars	
MMO 3614	Play The Blues Guitar: Dick Weissman	
MMO 3615	Orchestral Gems for Classical Guitar	
MMO 3616	**RODRIGO Concierto de Aranjuez (2CD)**	
MMO 3617	**GIULIANI Guitar Concerto No. 1 A major, op. 30 (2CD)**	
MMO 3619	**PIAZZOLLA Histoire du Tango**	
MMO 3620	Cool Jazz for Guitar	
MMO 3633	Sor: Classic guitar duos (intermediate) (2CD) (Avail. 17 Mar)	

Harp

MMO 5201	**MOZART Concerto Flt & Hrp C major K299 (2CD)**

Music & Musicians

MMO 7001	Rutgers University Music Dictation (7CD)
MMO 7004	Evolution of the Blues
MMO 7005	Art Of Improvisation, v. I
MMO 7006	Art Of Improvisation, v. II
MMO 7007	The Blues Minus You
MMO 7008	Take a Chorus
MMO 7009	Understanding Jazz
MMO 7010	Twelve Classic Jazz Standards
MMO 7011	Twelve More Classic Jazz Standards
MMO 7012	**Jazz Improv: complete course (5CD)**

Oboe

MMO 3356	Renaissance Dances and Fantasias
MMO 3358	Eighteenth Century Recorder Music (2 CD)
MMO 3359	English Consort Music (2 CD)
MMO 3400	**ALBINONI Oboe Concerti B-flat, op. 7 no. 3; D major, op. 7, no. 6; D min, op. 9, no. 2 (Remastered/2CD)**
MMO 3401	**Oboe Concerti: TELEMANN F minor; HÄNDEL B-flat; VIVALDI D minor (Remastered/2CD)**
MMO 3402	MOZART Quartet F major, KV370 (KV368b); STAMITZ Quartet F major, op. 8, no. 3 (Remastered/2CD) (Avail. 07 Apr)
MMO 3403	J.S. BACH Brandenburg Concerto No. 2; TELEMANN Concerto Am
MMO 3405	Masterpieces for Woodwind Quintet
MMO 3406	The Joy of Woodwind Quintets
MMO 3407	PEPUSCH Trio Sonata C major; TELEMANN Trio Sonata C minor
MMO 3408	QUANTZ Trio Sonata C minor; BACH Gigue ; BACH Trio Sonata G minor
MMO 3409	BEETHOVEN Quintet in E-flat major, op. 16
MMO 3411	Oboe Classics For Beginner
MMO 3412	Oboe Classics For The Intermediate Player
MMO 3413	**Oboe Classics For The Advanced Player**

Piano

MMO 2045	**2+2=5: A Study Odd Times**
MMO 3001	**BEETHOVEN Concerto No. 1, op. 15 (Remastered/2CD)**
MMO 3002	BEETHOVEN Concerto No. 2, op. 19
MMO 3004	BEETHOVEN Concerto No. 4, op. 58
MMO 3006	GRIEG Concerto A minor, op.16 (Remastered)
MMO 3007	**RACHMANINOV Concerto No. 2, op. 18 (Remastered/2CD)**
MMO 3008	SCHUMANN Concerto A minor, op. 54 (Remastered)
MMO 3009	BRAHMS Concerto No. 1 D minor (2 CD)
MMO 3010	**CHOPIN Concerto E minor, op. 11 (Remastered/3CD)**
MMO 3011	MENDELSSOHN Concerto No. 1 G minor, op. 25
MMO 5012	MOZART Concerto No. 9 E-flat, KV271
MMO 5013	MOZART Concerto No. 12 A major, KV414
MMO 3014	**MOZART Concerto No. 20 D minor, KV466 (Remastered/2CD)**
MMO 3016	MOZART Concerto No. 24 C minor, KV491
MMO 3017	**MOZART Concerto No. 26 D major, KV537 (Remastered/2CD)**
MMO 3018	MOZART Concerto No. 17 G major, KV453
MMO 3019	LISZT Concerto No. 1; WEBER Konzertstück
MMO 3020	LISZT Concerto No. 2; LISZT Hng. Fantasia
MMO 3021	**J.S. BACH Concerto F min, BWV1056; J.C.Fr. BACH Concerto E-flat (Remastered/2CD)**
MMO 3022	J.S. BACH Concerto D minor, BWV1052 (Remastered/2CD) (Avail. 07 Apr)
MMO 3023	HAYDN Concerto D major, HobXVIII/11
MMO 3024	The Heart of the Concerto
MMO 3025	Themes from Great Piano Concerti
MMO 3026	**TCHAIKOVSKY Concerto No. 1, op. 23 (Remastered/2CD)**
MMO 3027	RACHMANINOV Six Scenes
MMO 3028	ARENSKY 6 Pièces Enfantines, op. 34; STRAVINSKY 3 Easy Pieces
MMO 3029	FAURE 'Dolly' Suite, op. 56 (1P/4H duet)
MMO 3030	DEBUSSY Petite Suite (1P/4H duet)
MMO 3031	SCHUMANN 'Bilder aus Osten', op. 66; Children's Ball, op. 130
MMO 3032	BEETHOVEN Three Marches (1P/4H)
MMO 3033	Art of Popular Piano Playing, v. I
MMO 3034	Art of Popular Piano Playing, v. II (2CD)
MMO 3036	**MOZART Complete Music 1P/4H (2 CD)**
MMO 3037	DVORAK 'Dumky' Trio A maj, op. 90
MMO 3038	DVORAK Quintet A major, op. 81

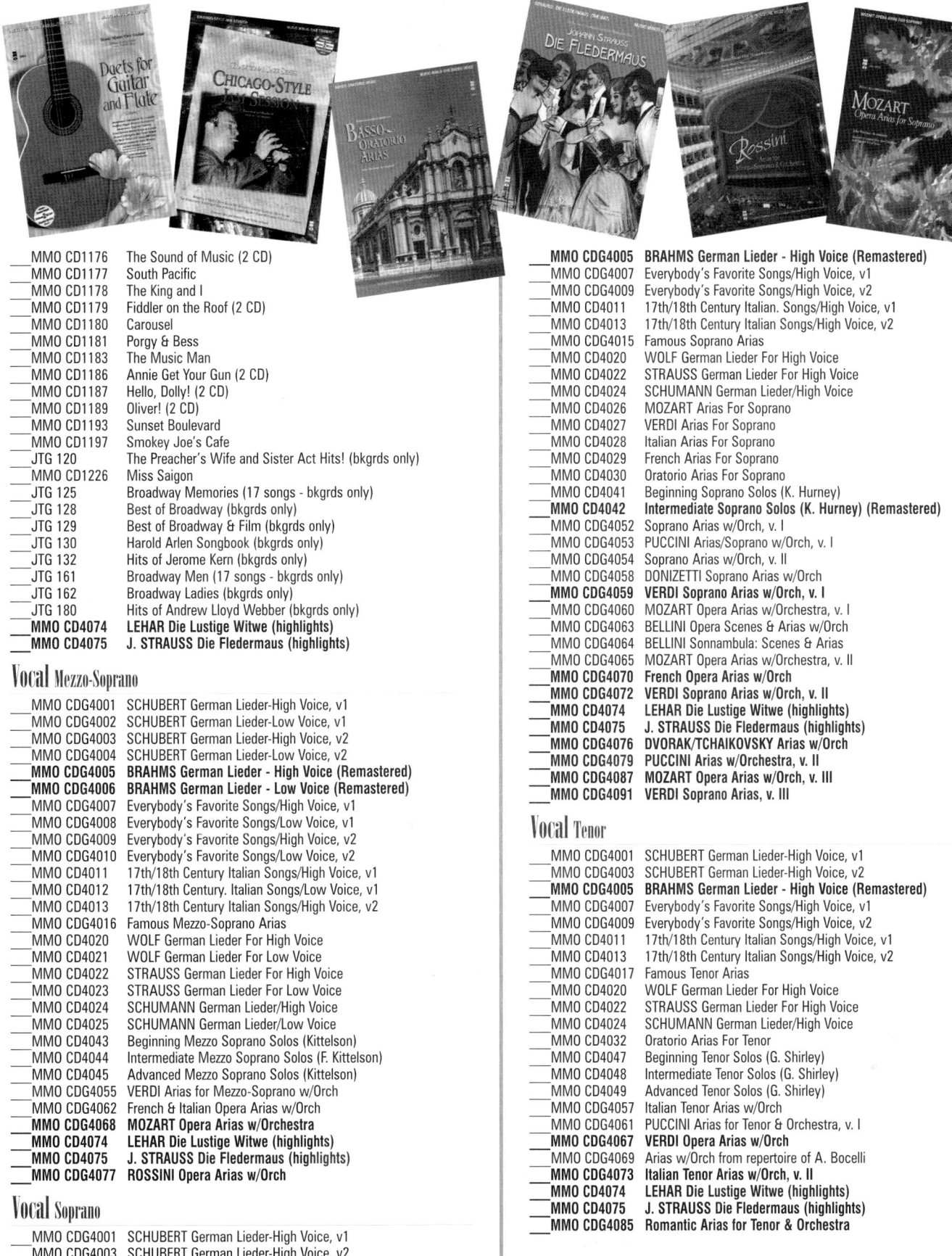

MMO CD1176	The Sound of Music (2 CD)	
MMO CD1177	South Pacific	
MMO CD1178	The King and I	
MMO CD1179	Fiddler on the Roof (2 CD)	
MMO CD1180	Carousel	
MMO CD1181	Porgy & Bess	
MMO CD1183	The Music Man	
MMO CD1186	Annie Get Your Gun (2 CD)	
MMO CD1187	Hello, Dolly! (2 CD)	
MMO CD1189	Oliver! (2 CD)	
MMO CD1193	Sunset Boulevard	
MMO CD1197	Smokey Joe's Cafe	
JTG 120	The Preacher's Wife and Sister Act Hits! (bkgrds only)	
MMO CD1226	Miss Saigon	
JTG 125	Broadway Memories (17 songs - bkgrds only)	
JTG 128	Best of Broadway (bkgrds only)	
JTG 129	Best of Broadway & Film (bkgrds only)	
JTG 130	Harold Arlen Songbook (bkgrds only)	
JTG 132	Hits of Jerome Kern (bkgrds only)	
JTG 161	Broadway Men (17 songs - bkgrds only)	
JTG 162	Broadway Ladies (bkgrds only)	
JTG 180	Hits of Andrew Lloyd Webber (bkgrds only)	
MMO CD4074	**LEHAR Die Lustige Witwe (highlights)**	
MMO CD4075	**J. STRAUSS Die Fledermaus (highlights)**	

Vocal Mezzo-Soprano

MMO CDG4001	SCHUBERT German Lieder-High Voice, v1	
MMO CDG4002	SCHUBERT German Lieder-Low Voice, v1	
MMO CDG4003	SCHUBERT German Lieder-High Voice, v2	
MMO CDG4004	SCHUBERT German Lieder-Low Voice, v2	
MMO CDG4005	**BRAHMS German Lieder - High Voice (Remastered)**	
MMO CDG4006	**BRAHMS German Lieder - Low Voice (Remastered)**	
MMO CDG4007	Everybody's Favorite Songs/High Voice, v1	
MMO CDG4008	Everybody's Favorite Songs/Low Voice, v1	
MMO CDG4009	Everybody's Favorite Songs/High Voice, v2	
MMO CDG4010	Everybody's Favorite Songs/Low Voice, v2	
MMO CD4011	17th/18th Century Italian Songs/High Voice, v1	
MMO CD4012	17th/18th Century. Italian Songs/Low Voice, v1	
MMO CD4013	17th/18th Century Italian Songs/High Voice, v2	
MMO CDG4016	Famous Mezzo-Soprano Arias	
MMO CD4020	WOLF German Lieder For High Voice	
MMO CD4021	WOLF German Lieder For Low Voice	
MMO CD4022	STRAUSS German Lieder For High Voice	
MMO CD4023	STRAUSS German Lieder For Low Voice	
MMO CD4024	SCHUMANN German Lieder/High Voice	
MMO CD4025	SCHUMANN German Lieder/Low Voice	
MMO CD4043	Beginning Mezzo Soprano Solos (Kittelson)	
MMO CD4044	Intermediate Mezzo Soprano Solos (F. Kittelson)	
MMO CD4045	Advanced Mezzo Soprano Solos (Kittelson)	
MMO CDG4055	VERDI Arias for Mezzo-Soprano w/Orch	
MMO CDG4062	French & Italian Opera Arias w/Orch	
MMO CDG4068	**MOZART Opera Arias w/Orchestra**	
MMO CD4074	**LEHAR Die Lustige Witwe (highlights)**	
MMO CD4075	**J. STRAUSS Die Fledermaus (highlights)**	
MMO CDG4077	**ROSSINI Opera Arias w/Orch**	

Vocal Soprano

MMO CDG4001	SCHUBERT German Lieder-High Voice, v1	
MMO CDG4003	SCHUBERT German Lieder-High Voice, v2	

MMO CDG4005	**BRAHMS German Lieder - High Voice (Remastered)**	
MMO CDG4007	Everybody's Favorite Songs/High Voice, v1	
MMO CDG4009	Everybody's Favorite Songs/High Voice, v2	
MMO CD4011	17th/18th Century Italian. Songs/High Voice, v1	
MMO CD4013	17th/18th Century Italian Songs/High Voice, v2	
MMO CDG4015	Famous Soprano Arias	
MMO CD4020	WOLF German Lieder For High Voice	
MMO CD4022	STRAUSS German Lieder For High Voice	
MMO CD4024	SCHUMANN German Lieder/High Voice	
MMO CD4026	MOZART Arias For Soprano	
MMO CD4027	VERDI Arias For Soprano	
MMO CD4028	Italian Arias For Soprano	
MMO CD4029	French Arias For Soprano	
MMO CD4030	Oratorio Arias For Soprano	
MMO CD4041	Beginning Soprano Solos (K. Hurney)	
MMO CD4042	**Intermediate Soprano Solos (K. Hurney) (Remastered)**	
MMO CDG4052	Soprano Arias w/Orch, v. I	
MMO CDG4053	PUCCINI Arias/Soprano w/Orch, v. I	
MMO CDG4054	Soprano Arias w/Orch, v. II	
MMO CDG4058	DONIZETTI Soprano Arias w/Orch	
MMO CDG4059	**VERDI Soprano Arias w/Orch, v. I**	
MMO CDG4060	MOZART Opera Arias w/Orchestra, v. I	
MMO CDG4063	BELLINI Opera Scenes & Arias w/Orch	
MMO CDG4064	BELLINI Sonnambula: Scenes & Arias	
MMO CDG4065	MOZART Opera Arias w/Orchestra, v. II	
MMO CDG4070	**French Opera Arias w/Orch**	
MMO CDG4072	**VERDI Soprano Arias w/Orch, v. II**	
MMO CD4074	**LEHAR Die Lustige Witwe (highlights)**	
MMO CD4075	**J. STRAUSS Die Fledermaus (highlights)**	
MMO CDG4076	**DVORAK/TCHAIKOVSKY Arias w/Orch**	
MMO CDG4079	**PUCCINI Arias w/Orchestra, v. II**	
MMO CDG4087	**MOZART Opera Arias w/Orch, v. III**	
MMO CDG4091	**VERDI Soprano Arias, v. III**	

Vocal Tenor

MMO CDG4001	SCHUBERT German Lieder-High Voice, v1	
MMO CDG4003	SCHUBERT German Lieder-High Voice, v2	
MMO CDG4005	**BRAHMS German Lieder - High Voice (Remastered)**	
MMO CDG4007	Everybody's Favorite Songs/High Voice, v1	
MMO CDG4009	Everybody's Favorite Songs/High Voice, v2	
MMO CD4011	17th/18th Century Italian Songs/High Voice, v1	
MMO CD4013	17th/18th Century Italian Songs/High Voice, v2	
MMO CD4017	Famous Tenor Arias	
MMO CD4020	WOLF German Lieder For High Voice	
MMO CD4022	STRAUSS German Lieder For High Voice	
MMO CD4024	SCHUMANN German Lieder/High Voice	
MMO CD4032	Oratorio Arias For Tenor	
MMO CD4047	Beginning Tenor Solos (G. Shirley)	
MMO CD4048	Intermediate Tenor Solos (G. Shirley)	
MMO CD4049	Advanced Tenor Solos (G. Shirley)	
MMO CDG4057	Italian Tenor Arias w/Orch	
MMO CDG4061	PUCCINI Arias for Tenor & Orchestra, v. I	
MMO CDG4067	**VERDI Opera Arias w/Orch**	
MMO CDG4069	Arias w/Orch from repertoire of A. Bocelli	
MMO CDG4073	**Italian Tenor Arias w/Orch, v. II**	
MMO CD4074	**LEHAR Die Lustige Witwe (highlights)**	
MMO CD4075	**J. STRAUSS Die Fledermaus (highlights)**	
MMO CDG4085	**Romantic Arias for Tenor & Orchestra**	

MMO Music Group • 50 Executive Boulevard • Elmsford, New York 10523
1-800-669-7464 (U.S.) • 914-592-1188 (Int'l)

www.musicminusone.com • e-mail: **mmogroup@musicminusone.com**

Boldface=Recent or Upcoming Release • Street Dates Subject To Change   January 2003

___	MMO 3039	MENDELSSOHN Trio No. 1 in D, op. 49
___	MMO 3040	MENDELSSOHN Trio No. 2 C minor, op. 66
___	MMO 3041	MAYKAPAR First Steps, op. 29
___	MMO 3042	TCHAIKOVSKY 50 Russian Folk Songs
___	MMO 3043	BIZET Jeux d'enfants, op. 22
___	MMO 3044	GRETCHANINOV On Green Meadow
___	MMO 3045	POZZOLI Smiles of Childhood
___	MMO 3046	DIABELLI Pleasures of Youth, op. 163
___	MMO 3047	SCHUBERT Fantasie F minor, op. 103; Grand Sonata B-flat, op. 30
___	MMO 3049	Blues Fusion for Piano
___	MMO 3050	BOLLING Suite for Flute and Jazz Trio
___	MMO 3053	From Dixie to Swing
___	MMO 3054	J.S. BACH Brandenburg Concerto 5 BWV1050
___	MMO 3055	J.S. BACH Concerto 2 pianos C minor, BWV1060; SCHUMANN Andante & Vars.
___	MMO 3056	HÄNDEL Concerto Grosso D major, op. 3, no. 6; HAYDN Concertino C major; J.C. BACH Concerto B-flat major, op.13, no. 4
___	MMO3057	J.S. BACH 'Triple' Concerto A minor, BWV1044; Brandenburg No. 5 (1st mvmt)
___	MMO 3058	MENDELSSOHN Capriccio Brilliant; FRANCK Variations Symphoniques
___	MMO 3059	C.P.E. BACH Concerto A minor, Wq26, H430
___	MMO 3060	STRETCHIN' OUT
___	MMO 3061	RAVEL Trio A min
___	MMO 3064	SCHUMANN Trio D minor, op. 63
___	**MMO 3065**	**BEETHOVEN Trio No. 8 E-flat, WoO38; Trio No. 11 G major ('Kakadu'), op. 121a (Remastered)**
___	MMO 3066	SCHUBERT Trio B-flat, op. 99, (2 CD)
___	MMO 3067	SCHUBERT Trio E-flat, op. 100, (2 CD)
___	MMO 3070	BEETHOVEN Quintet E-flat major, op. 16
___	MMO 3071	MOZART Quintet E-flat major, KV452
___	**MMO 3072**	**MOZART Concerto No. 21 C major, KV467 (2CD)**
___	MMO 3073	MOZART Concerto No. 14 E-flat major, KV449
___	**MMO 3074**	**RACHMANINOV Concerto 3, op.30 (3CD)**
___	**MMO 3075**	**CHOPIN Concerto F minor, op. 21 (2CD)**
___	MMO 3076	HAYDN Trios, v. II: G major (HobXV:25); F#minor (HobXV:26); F(HobXV:6)
___	**MMO 3078**	**GLAZUNOV Concerto No. 1 F minor, op. 92 (2CD)**
___	**MMO 3079**	**RUBINSTEIN Concerto No. 4 D minor, op. 70 (2CD)**
___	**MMO 3080**	**ARENSKY Concerto F major, op. 2 (2CD)**
___	**MMO 3081**	**MOZART Concerto No. 19 F major, KV459 (2CD)**
___	**MMO 3082**	**MOZART Concerto No. 27 B-flat major, KV595 (2CD)**
___	**MMO 3083**	**GERSHWIN Rhapsody in Blue**
___	**MMO 3084**	**RACHMANINOV Rhapsody on a Theme of Paganini (2CD)**
___	**MMO 3086**	**RIMSKY-KORSAKOV Concerto C# minor, op. 30; ARENSKY Fantasia, op. 48 (2CD)**
___	MMO 3087	SCHUBERT Quintet A major, op. 114, 'Trout'
___	**MMO 3090**	**MACDOWELL Concerto No. 2 D minor, op. 23 (2CD)**
___	**MMO 3091**	**C.P.E. BACH Concerto D minor, Wq23 (2CD)**
___	**MMO 3092**	**MOZART Concerto No. 25 C major, KV503 (2CD)**
___	**MMO 3098**	**MOZART Concerto No. 23 in A, KV488 (New Recording/2CD)**
___	**MMO 3099**	**MOZART Concerto #5 in D K175/Rondo K382 (2CD)**
___	**MMO 6003**	**BEETHOVEN Conc. No. 3 C minor, op. 37 (New Recording - 2CD)**
___	**MMO 6005**	**BEETHOVEN Conc. No. 5 E-flat, op. 73 (New Recording - 2CD)**
___	**MMO 6016**	**MOZART Conc. No.1 F maj, KV37; Conc. No.3 D maj, KV40 (2CD)**

Recorder

___	MMO 3339	You Can Play the Recorder: Begining (Adult)

Recorder (alto)

___	MMO 3306	J.S. BACH Brandenburg Concerto No. 2 F major; HAYDN Flute Concerto No. 9 D minor
___	MMO 3310	J.S. BACH Brandenburg Concerti Nos. 4 in G (BWV1049) & 5 in D (BWV1050)
___	MMO 3312	TELEMANN Suite A minor; GLUCK 'Orfee' scene; PERGOLESI Concerto in G (2CD) (Avail. 17 Mar)
___	MMO 3314	VIVALDI Flute Concerti D major (RV427); F major (RV434); G major (RV438)
___	MMO 3340	3 Sonatas (Händel & Telemann)

___	MMO 3341	3 Sonatas (Telemann, Händel & Marcello)
___	MMO 3346	PEPUSCH Sonata C; TELEMANN Sonata C minor
___	MMO 3349	TELEMANN Trio F major; B-flat; HÄNDEL Sonata No. 3 C major
___	MMO 3350	HÄNDEL; MARCELLO; TELEMANN Sonatas F major
___	MMO 3357	Echoes of Time (2 CD)
___	MMO 3358	Eighteenth Century Recorder Music (2 CD)
___	MMO 3360	Dances of Three Centuries
___	MMO 3370	VERACINI Four Sonatas

Recorder (bass)

___	MMO 3360	Dances of Three Centuries

Recorder (soprano)

___	MMO 3337	Playing the Recorder: Folk Songs
___	MMO 3338	Let's Play the Recorder: Begining. (Children)
___	MMO 3356	Renaissance Dances and Fantasias
___	MMO 3357	Echoes of Time (2 CD)
___	MMO 3359	English Consort Music (2 CD)
___	MMO 3360	Dances of Three Centuries

Recorder (tenor)

___	MMO 3359	English Consort Music (2 CD)
___	MMO 3360	Dances of Three Centuries

Saxophone (alto)

___	**MMO 2041**	**2+2=5: A Study Odd Times**
___	MMO 3218	Jazz Standards w/Rhythm Section (2 CD)
___	MMO 3219	Jazz Standards with Strings (2 CD)
___	MMO 4101	Alto Saxophone Solos: Student Ed., v. I
___	MMO 4102	Alto Saxophone Solos: Student Ed., v. II
___	MMO 4103	Easy Jazz Duets 2 Alto Saxes/Rhythm Section
___	MMO 4104	For Saxes Only: Bob Wilber
___	MMO 4108	Stompin' & Struttin' the New Swing
___	MMO 4111	Beginning Alto Sax Solos, v. I (P. Brodie)
___	MMO 4112	Beginning Alto Sax Solos, v. II (V. Abato)
___	MMO 4113	Intermediate Alto Sax Solos, v. I (P. Brodie)
___	MMO 4114	Intermediate Alto Sax Solos, v. II (V. Abato)
___	MMO 4115	Advanced Alto Sax Solos, v. I (P. Brodie)
___	MMO 4116	Advanced Alto Sax Solos, v. II (V. Abato)
___	MMO 4117	Advanced Alto Sax Solos, v. III (P. Brodie)
___	MMO 4118	Advanced Alto Sax Solos, v. IV (V. Abato)
___	MMO 4119	Teacher's Partner: Basic Studies
___	MMO 4120	Play Lead a Sax Section: Bob Wilber
___	MMO 4121	Days of Wine & Roses/Sensual Sax
___	MMO 4126	Popular Concert Favorites with Orchestra
___	MMO 4127	Band Aids: Concert Band Favorites
___	MMO 4128	Music for Saxophone Quartet
___	MMO 4129	World Favorites: 41 Easy Selections
___	MMO 4130	Classic Themes: 27 Easy Songs
___	MMO 4132	GLAZUNOV & VON KOCH Concerti
___	MMO 4205	Bluesaxe: Blues for Saxophone
___	MMO 4209	Play Lead a Sax Section: The Bob Wilber All-Stars
___	MMO 4210	Days of Wine & Roses
___	MMO 4216	Cool Jazz (Rich Maraday)
___	MMO 4217	Sinatra, Sax and Swing (Brian Hayes)
___	MMO 7010	Twelve Classic Jazz Standards
___	MMO 7011	Twelve More Classic Jazz Standards

Saxophone (baritone)

___	MMO 4104	For Saxes Only: Bob Wilber
___	MMO 4205	Bluesaxe: Blues for Saxophone
___	MMO 4209	Play Lead a Sax Section: The Bob Wilber All-Stars
___	MMO 4210	Days of Wine & Roses
___	MMO 4901	Music for Saxophone Quartet
___	MMO 4902	Stompin' & Struttin' the New Swing
___	MMO 7010	Twelve Classic Jazz Standards
___	MMO 7011	Twelve More Classic Jazz Standards

Saxophone (soprano)

- MMO 4205 Bluesaxe: Blues for Saxophone
- MMO 4209 Play Lead a Sax Section: The Bob Wilber All-Stars
- MMO 4210 Days of Wine & Roses
- MMO 4801 Music for Saxophone Quartet
- MMO 4802 Stompin' & Struttin' the New Swing
- MMO 7010 Twelve Classic Jazz Standards
- MMO 7011 Twelve More Classic Jazz Standards

Saxophone (tenor)

- **MMO 2042 2+2=5: A Study Odd Times**
- MMO 3218 Jazz Standards w/Rhythm Section (2 CD)
- MMO 3219 Jazz Standards with Strings (2 CD)
- MMO 3829 When Jazz Was Young: Bob Wilber
- MMO 4201 Easy Tenor Saxophone Solos: vol. I
- MMO 4202 Easy Tenor Saxophone Solos: vol. II
- MMO 4203 Easy Jazz Duets 2 Tenor Saxes/Rhythm Section
- MMO 4204 For Saxes Only: Bob Wilber
- MMO 4205 Bluesaxe: Blues for Saxophone
- MMO 4209 Play Lead a Sax Section: The Bob Wilber All-Stars
- MMO 4210 Days of Wine & Roses
- MMO 4211 Music for Saxophone Quartet
- MMO 4212 Popular Concert Favorites with Orchestra
- MMO 4213 Band Aids: Concert Band Favorites
- MMO 4214 Tenor Jazz Jam (2 CD)
- MMO 4215 Stompin' & Struttin' the New Swing
- MMO 4216 Cool Jazz (Rich Maraday)
- MMO 4217 Sinatra, Sax and Swing (Brian Hayes)
- **MMO 4218 Traditional Jazz Series: Chicago-Style Jam Session (2CD)**
- MMO 7010 Twelve Classic Jazz Standards
- MMO 7011 Twelve More Classic Jazz Standards

Trombone

- **MMO 2044 2+2=5: A Study Odd Times**
- MMO 3901 Easy Trombone Solos: Student Level, v. I
- MMO 3902 Easy Trombone Solos: Student Level, v. II
- MMO 3903 Easy Jazz Duets: 2 Trombs & Rhythm Section
- MMO 3904 Baroque Brass and Beyond: Quintets
- MMO 3905 Music for Brass Ensemble
- MMO 3907 Big Band Ballads: Tenor or Bass Trombone
- MMO 3908 STRAVINSKY L'Histoire du Soldat
- MMO 3909 Classical Trombone Solos (2 CD)
- MMO 3910 Jazz Standards with Strings (2 CD)
- MMO 3911 Beginning Trombone Solos, v. I (P. Brevig)
- MMO 3912 Beginning Trombone Solos, v. II (J. Friedman)
- MMO 3913 Intermediate Trombone Solos, v. I (K. Brown)
- MMO 3914 Intermediate Trombone Solos, v. II (J. Friedman)
- MMO 3915 Advanced Trombone Solos, v. I (K. Brown)
- MMO 3916 Advanced Trombone Solos, v. II (P. Brevig)
- MMO 3917 Advanced Trombone Solos, v. III (K. Brown)
- MMO 3918 Advanced Trombone Solos, v. IV (J. Friedman)
- MMO 3919 Advanced Trombone Solos, v. V (P. Brevig)
- MMO 3920 Teacher's Partner: Basic Studies
- **MMO 3921 Traditional Jazz Series: Chicago-Style Jam Session (2CD)**
- MMO 3926 From Dixie to Swing
- MMO 3927 Sticks & Bones: Brass Quintets
- MMO 3928 For Trombones Only: More Brass Quintets
- MMO 3929 Popular Concert Favorites with Orchestra
- MMO 3930 Band Aids: Concert Band Favorites
- MMO 3931 World Favorites: 41 Easy Selections
- MMO 3932 Classic Themes: 27 Easy Songs
- MMO 7010 Twelve Classic Jazz Standards
- MMO 7011 Twelve More Classic Jazz Standards

Trumpet in B-flat

- **MMO 2043 2+2=5: A Study Odd Times**
- **MMO 3801 HAYDN Concerto in E-flat, HobVIIe:1; TELEMANN Concerto in D; FASCH Concerto in D (Remastered/2CD)**
- MMO 3802 Trumpet Solos: Student Level, v. I
- MMO 3803 Trumpet Solos: Student Level, v. II
- MMO 3804 Easy Jazz Duets 2 Trumpets/Rhythm Section
- MMO 3805 Music for Brass Ensemble
- MMO 3806 First Chair Trumpet Solos with Orchestra
- MMO 3807 Art of the Solo Trumpet with Orchestra
- MMO 3808 Baroque Brass and Beyond: Quintets
- MMO 3809 Complete Arban Duets
- MMO 3810 SOUSA Marches plus BEETHOVEN, BERLIOZ, STRAUSS
- MMO 3811 Beginning Contest Solos, v. I (G. Schwarz)
- MMO 3812 Beginning Contest Solos, v. II (A. Ghitalla)
- MMO 3813 Intermediate Trumpet Solos, v. I (R. Nagel)

- MMO 3814 Intermediate Trumpet Solos, v. II (G. Schwarz)
- MMO 3815 Advanced Trumpet Solos, v. I (R. Nagel)
- MMO 3816 Intermediate Trumpet Solos, v. IV (A. Ghitalla)
- MMO 3817 Intermediate Trumpet Solos, v. III (G. Schwarz)
- MMO 3818 Advanced Trumpet Solos, v. II (R. Nagel)
- MMO 3819 Advanced Trumpet Solos, v. III (A. Ghitalla)
- MMO 3820 Beginning Trumpet Solos, v. III (R. Crisara)
- MMO 3821 Beginning Trumpet Solos, v. IV (R. Crisara)
- MMO 3822 Intermediate Trumpet Solos, v. V (R. Crisara)
- MMO 3823 Teacher's Partner: Basic Trumpet Studies
- MMO 3826 From Dixie to Swing
- MMO 3827 Trumpet Pieces: Brass Quintets
- MMO 3828 Modern Brass Quintets
- MMO 3829 When Jazz Was Young: Bob Wilber
- MMO 3830 Classic Trumpet Solos with Piano
- MMO 3831 Popular Concert Favorites Trumpet with Orchestra
- MMO 3832 Band Aids: Concert Band Favorites with Orchestra
- MMO 3835 STRAVINSKY L'Histoire du Soldat
- MMO 3836 World Favorites: 41 Easy Selections
- MMO 3837 Classic Themes: 27 Easy Songs
- MMO 3838 Stompin' & Struttin' the New Swing
- MMO 3840 Classic Pieces for Trumpet & Organ (2CD)
- **MMO 3844 Traditional Jazz Series: Chicago-Style Jam Session (2CD)**
- MMO 4104 For Saxes Only: Bob Wilber
- MMO 4205 Bluesaxe: Blues for Saxophone
- MMO 4209 Play Lead a Sax Section: The Bob Wilber All-Stars
- MMO 4210 Days of Wine & Roses
- MMO 7010 Twelve Classic Jazz Standards
- MMO 7011 Twelve More Classic Jazz Standards

Tuba/Bass Trombone

- MMO 4701 He's Not Heavy, He's My Tuba
- MMO 4702 Sweets for Brass
- MMO 4703 Music for Brass Ensemble

Vibraphone (Vibes)

- MMO 5101 For Vibists Only!: Shelly Elias Method, v1
- MMO 5102 Good Vibe-rations: Shelly Elias Method, v2

Viol (treble)/Discant

- MMO 3359 English Consort Music (2 CD)

Viola

- **MMO 4501 Viola Solos with piano accompaniment (Remastered/2CD)**
- MMO 4502 DVORAK String Trio C major, op. 74, B148
- MMO 4503 BEETHOVEN Quartet A minor,op.132 (2CD)
- MMO 4504 DVORAK Quintet A major, op. 81
- MMO 4505 HOFFMEISTER Concerto D major
- MMO 4506 SCHUBERT Quintet A major, op. 114, 'Trout'

Violin

- MMO 3100 BRUCH Vln Concerto No. 1 G minor, op. 26
- **MMO 3101 MENDELSSOHN Vln Concerto E minor, op. 64 (Remastered/2CD)**
- MMO 3102 TCHAIKOVSKY Violin Concerto D major, op. 35
- MMO 3103 J.S. BACH 'Double' Concerto D minor, BWV1043
- MMO 3104 J.S. BACH Vln Concerto No. 1 A minor, BWV1041; Vln Concerto No. 2 E major, BWV1042 (Remastered/2CD) (Avail. 17 Mar)
- MMO 3105 J.S. BACH Brandenburg Cti Nos. 4 G major (BWV1048) & 5 D major (BWV1050)
- MMO 3106 J.S. BACH Brandenburg Conc. No. 2; 'Triple' Conc. A min, BWV1044
- MMO 3107 J.S. BACH Violin Concerto D minor
- MMO 3108 BRAHMS Vln Concerto D major, op. 77
- MMO 3109 CHAUSSON Poëme, op. 25; SCHUBERT Rondo, D438
- MMO 3110 LALO Symphonie Espagnole, op. 21
- MMO 3111 MOZART Vln Conc. 4, KV218; VIVALDI Conc. A minor, op.3 no.6
- MMO 3113 WIENIAWSKI Violin Concerto No. 2 D minor, op. 22; SARASATE Zigeunerweisen, op. 20
- MMO 3114 VIOTTI Violin Concerto 22 A minor
- MMO 3115 BEETHOVEN Two Romances; Sonata No. 5 F major, 'Spring'
- MMO 3116 SAINT-SAËNS Intro/Rondo Capriccioso; MOZART Serenade #5 K204; Adagio K261
- **MMO 3117 BEETHOVEN Violin Concerto D op. 61 (Remastered/2 CD)**
- MMO 3118 The Concertmaster: Symphonic Solos
- MMO 3119 Air on a G String: Favorite Encores w/Orch
- **MMO 3120 Concert Pieces for the Serious Violinist (Remastered/2CD)**
- MMO 3121 18th Century Pieces Vln & Orch
- **MMO 3122 Easy Concert Pieces Vln & Orch**
- MMO 3123 Orchestral Favorites, v.2 (Intermediate Level)
- MMO 3124 Orchestral Favorites, v.3 (Intermediate-Difficult)
- MMO 3125 The Three Bs: Bach/Beethoven/Brahms

	MMO 3126	VIVALDI Concerto A minor, op. 3, no. 6, RV356; Concerto Grosso A minor, op.3, no. 8, RV522; Concerto D major op. 3, no.9, RV230
	MMO 3127	VIVALDI 'Le Quattre Stagioni' ('The Four Seasons'), op. 8, nos. 1-4 (2 CD)
	MMO 3128	VIVALDI Violin Concerto E-flat major, op. 8, no. 5, RV253; ALBINONI Violin Concerto A major
	MMO 3129	VIVALDI Violin Concerto E major, op. 3, no. 12, RV265; C major, op. 8, no.6, RV180
	MMO 3130	SCHUBERT Three Sonatinas (R. Zubrycki)
	MMO 3131	HAYDN Quartet G major, op.76/1, HobIII:75
	MMO 3132	HAYDN Quartet Dminor, op.76/2, HobIII:76
	MMO 3133	HAYDN Quartet C major, op. 76/3, HobIII:77
	MMO 3134	HAYDN Quartet B-flt, op. 76/4, HobIII:78
	MMO 3135	HAYDN Quartet D major, op. 76/5, HobIII:79
	MMO 3136	HAYDN Quartet E-flt, op. 76/6, HobIII:80
	MMO 3137	Beautiful Music for Two Violins, v. I: 1st pos.
	MMO 3138	Beautiful Music for Two Violins, v. II: 2nd pos.
	MMO 3139	Beautiful Music for Two Violins, v. III: 3rd pos.
	MMO 3140	**Beautiful Music for Two Violins, v. IV: 1st, 2nd, 3rd pos. (2CD)**
	MMO 3141	The Heart of the Violin Concerto
	MMO 3142	Teacher's Partner: Studies, 1st year
	MMO 3143	DVORAK String Trio 'Terzetto' C maj, op. 74, B148 (2 Vlns & viola)
	MMO 3144	SIBELIUS Violin Concerto D minor, op. 47
	MMO 3145	Themes from the major Violin Concerti
	MMO 3146	STRAVINSKY L'Histoire du Soldat
	MMO 3147	RAVEL Trio A minor
	MMO 3151	Great Scott: Joplin's Ragtime Quartets
	MMO 3152	SCHUMANN Trio D minor, op. 63
	MMO 3153	BEETHOVEN Trio No. 8 E-flat major, WoO 38, & No. 11 G major, 'Kakadu,' op. 121a
	MMO 3154	SCHUBERT Trio B-flat major, op. 99, (2CD)
	MMO 3155	SCHUBERT Trio E-flat, op. 100, (2CD)
	MMO 3156	BEETHOVEN Quartet A minor, op.132 (2CD)
	MMO 3157	DVORAK Quintet A major, op. 81
	MMO 3158	BEETHOVEN Quartets, op. 18: No. 1 F major & No. 4 C minor
	MMO 3159	HAYDN Trios, v. I: F major (HobXV:17), D major (HobXV:16), and G major (HobXV:15)
	MMO 3160	MOZART Violin Concerto No. 3 G major, KV216
	MMO 3161	**MOZART Violin Concerto No. 1 B-flat major, KV207; Rondo Concertant B-flat major, KV269 (2CD)**
	MMO 3162	Mischa Elman Favorite Encores (2 CD)
	MMO 3163	Mischa Elman Concert Favorites (2 CD)
	MMO 3164	Jascha Heifitz Favorite Encores (2 CD)
	MMO 3165	KREISLER Favorite Encores (2 CD)
	MMO 3166	**KORNGOLD Violin Concerto D major, op. 35 (2CD)**
	MMO 3167	**MOZART Violin Concerto No. 2 D major, KV211 (2CD)**
	MMO 3168	**GLAZUNOV Violin Concerto A minor, op. 82 (2CD)**
	MMO 3169	SCHUBERT Quintet A major, op. 114, 'Trout'
	MMO 3171	**BRAHMS Double Concerto A minor, op. 102 (3CD)**
	MMO 3172	**BRUCH Violin Concerto No. 2 D minor, op. 44 (2CD)**
	MMO 3191	**VIVALDI 'La Stravaganza,' vol. I: Concerti, op. 4, nos. 1-2 (2CD)**
	MMO 3340	3 Sonatas (Händel & Telemann)
	MMO 3341	3 Sonatas (Telemann, Händel & Marcello)
	MMO 3347	QUANTZ Trio Sonata C minor; BACH Gigue; ABEL Sonata No. 2 F major
	MMO 3348	TELEMANN Concerto No. 1 D major/ CORRETTE Sonata E minor
	MMO 3356	Renaissance Dances and Fantasias
	MMO 3358	Eighteenth Century Recorder Music (2 CD)
	MMO 3359	English Consort Music (2 CD)
	MMO 3370	**VERACINI Four Sonatas**

Violoncello

	MMO 3701	DVORAK 'Cello Concerto B minor, op.104 (2 CD)
	MMO 3702	C.P.E. BACH Concerto A minor, Wq170/H432
	MMO 3703	BOCCHERINI 'Cello Concerto No. 9 B-flat major, G482; BRUCH Kol Nidrei, op. 47
	MMO 3704	Ten Concert Pieces for 'Cello and Piano
	MMO 3705	SCHUMANN Concerto A minor, op. 129
	MMO 3706	BOLLING Suite For 'Cello and Jazz Trio
	MMO 3707	RAVEL Trio A minor
	MMO 3708	Great Scott! Ragtime Minus You
	MMO 3709	SCHUMANN Trio No. 1 D minor, op. 63
	MMO 3710	BEETHOVEN Trio No. 8 E-flat major, WoO38 & Trio No. 11 G major, op. 121a
	MMO 3711	SCHUBERT Trio B-flat major, op. 99 (2 CD)
	MMO 3712	SCHUBERT Trio E-flat major, op. 100 (2CD)
	MMO 3713	BEETHOVEN Quartet A minor, op.132(2CD)
	MMO 3714	DVORAK Quintet A major, op. 81
	MMO 3715	BEETHOVEN 'Cello Sonata A major, op. 69; TELEMANN 'Cello Duet B-flat
	MMO 3716	WINER 'Cello Concerto; SCHUBERT Ave Maria; SAINT-SAENS Allegro Appass.

	MMO 3718	HAYDN 'Cello Concerto C major, HobVIIb:1 (2CD)
	MMO 3719	HAYDN 'Cello Concerto D major, HobVIIb:2 (2CD)
	MMO 3720	**ELGAR 'Cello Concerto E minor, op. 85 (2CD)**
	MMO 3721	SCHUBERT Quintet A major, op. 114, 'Trout'
	MMO 3722	**BRAHMS Double Concerto A minor, op. 102 (2CD)**
	MMO 3726	**The Cello Soloist: Classic Solos (2CD)**

Vocal Bass-Baritone

	MMO CDG4001	SCHUBERT German Lieder-High Voice, v1
	MMO CDG4002	SCHUBERT German Lieder-Low Voice, v1
	MMO CDG4003	SCHUBERT German Lieder-High Voice, v2
	MMO CDG4004	SCHUBERT German Lieder-Low Voice, v2
	MMO CDG4005	**BRAHMS German Lieder - High Voice (Remastered)**
	MMO CDG4006	**BRAHMS German Lieder - Low Voice (Remastered)**
	MMO CDG4007	Everybody's Favorite Songs/High Voice, v1
	MMO CDG4008	Everybody's Favorite Songs/Low Voice, v1
	MMO CDG4009	Everybody's Favorite Songs/High Voice, v2
	MMO CDG4010	Everybody's Favorite Songs/Low Voice, v2
	MMO CD4011	17th/18th Century Italian Songs/High Voice, v1
	MMO CD4012	17th/18th Century Italian Songs/Low Voice, v1
	MMO CD4013	17th/18th Century Italian Songs/High Voice, v2
	MMO CD4014	17th/18th Century Italian Songs/Low Voice, v2
	MMO CDG4018	Famous Baritone Arias
	MMO CDG4019	Famous Bass Arias
	MMO CD4020	WOLF German Lieder For High Voice
	MMO CD4021	WOLF German Lieder For Low Voice
	MMO CD4022	STRAUSS German Lieder For High Voice
	MMO CD4023	STRAUSS German Lieder For Low Voice
	MMO CD4024	SCHUMANN German Lieder/High Voice
	MMO CD4025	SCHUMANN German Lieder/Low Voice
	MMO CD4033	Oratorio Arias For Bass
	MMO CDG4056	Bass-Baritone Arias w/Orch, v. I
	MMO CDG4066	Bass-Baritone Arias w/Orch, v. II
	MMO CDG4071	**Italian Opera Arias w/Orchestra**
	MMO CD4074	**LEHAR Die Lustige Witwe (highlights)**
	MMO CD4075	**J. STRAUSS Die Fledermaus (highlights)**
	MMO CDG4078	**VERDI Bass-Baritone Arias w/Orch**
	MMO CDG4090	**Russian Opera Arias for Bass-Baritone**
	MMO CDG4093	MOZART Bass-Baritone Opera Arias w/Orchestra, v. I (Avail. 07 Apr)

Vocal Contralto

	MMO CDG4002	SCHUBERT German Lieder-Low Voice, v1
	MMO CDG4004	SCHUBERT German Lieder-Low Voice, v2
	MMO CDG4006	**BRAHMS German Lieder - Low Voice (Remastered)**
	MMO CDG4008	Everybody's Favorite Songs/Low Voice, v1
	MMO CDG4010	Everybody's Favorite Songs/Low Voice, v2
	MMO CD4012	17th/18th Century Italian Songs/Low Voice, v1
	MMO CD4021	WOLF German Lieder For Low Voice
	MMO CD4023	STRAUSS German Lieder For Low Voice
	MMO CD4025	SCHUMANN German Lieder/Low Voice
	MMO CD4031	Oratorio Arias For Contralto
	MMO CD4046	Beginning Contralto Solos (C. Ray)
	MMO CD4074	**LEHAR Die Lustige Witwe (highlights)**
	MMO CD4075	**J. STRAUSS Die Fledermaus (highlights)**

Vocal General

	JTG 020	Jekyll & Hyde/Scarlet Pimpernel (bkgrds only)
	JTG 021	**The Wiz (bkgrds only)**
	JTG 037	**Evita (bkgrds only)**
	JTG 038	**Jesus Christ Superstar! (bkgrds only)**
	JTG 039	**Songs of Andrew Lloyd Webber (bkgrds only)**
	JTG 048	**Cinderella! (bkgrds only)**
	JTG 049	**Pippin (bkgrds only)**
	JTG 056	**Hits of Rodgers & Hammerste(bkgrds only)**
	JTG 060	**Chess (bkgrds only)**
	JTG 063	**Bye Bye Birdie - The Film Version (bkgrds only)**
	MMO CDG1016	Les Miserables/Phantom of the Opera
	MMO CDG1067	Guys and Dolls
	MMO CD1100	West Side Story (2 CD)
	JTG 111	Wizard of Oz, Peter Pan, & the Animals (bkgrds only)
	MMO CD1110	Cabaret (2 CD)
	JTG 113	Let's Go To The Movies (bkgrds only)
	JTG 114	Disney's New Movies (bkgrds only)
	MMO CDG1151	Jekyll & Hyde
	MMO CD1160	Showboat
	JTG 117	Hits of Lerner & Loewe (bkgrds only)
	MMO CD1173	Camelot
	MMO CD1174	My Fair Lady (2 CD)
	MMO CD1175	Oklahoma!

MUSIC MINUS ONE

Participation Recordings for All Instrumentalists & Singers

2002

Index

About Music Minus One

Begun in 1950, MMO this year enters its 52nd year of continuous activity under the guidance of a single individual still active in guiding its programs. It has become an established part of the musician's world known to three generations of musicians, many still clients. Its catalog offers 700 titles on compact disc, with new recordings being added all the time.

MMO recordings provide musicians with a unique way to study, rehearse and perform with professional ensembles in the comfort of their own home. All types of music from jazz to chamber music as well as orchestral concerti are offered for all instruments. In recent years, the recordings have been augmented by adding professional soloists to each production. The user can now hear the solo part and then perform it themselves.

Everyone may now share the unique experience of having an ensemble at their disposal. Whether it be a thrilling symphony orchestra or a top-notch jazz rhythm section, MMO gives every musician the chance to perform with professional ensembles in their own living room.

Repertoire and Artists without Equal

MMO's repertoire is an amazing one: offering hundreds of albums ranging from classical baroque to 20th century modern, from vocal standards and jazz trios to rock-drumming and classical percussion primers, from Vivaldi's *Four Seasons* to Glazunov's 1934 *Saxophone Concerto,* from its inaugural 1950 recording of the Schubert *Trout Quintet* to its new ground-breaking *Opera with Orchestra* series, truly all-encompassing.

Superior Quality

All of MMO's latest releases feature newly engraved printed scores, on beautiful acid-free ivory paper, often in unique and authoritative, definitive editions with annotations and performance suggestions from world-class artists. Historical liner notes and biographical information on the composers and works add an extra dimension, allowing the soloist to gain insight into each work's genesis and history.

Unrivaled Convenience

Music Minus One editions offer limitless possibilities for practice, for developing artistry and technique. World-quality soloists and orchestras, new and definitive printed editions of classic works, and innovative technologies combine to make a product without rival, one that today's musicians can utilize to the fullest.

Music Minus One • 50 Executive Boulevard • Elmsford, New York 10523-1325
Visit our two websites: www.musicminusone.com and www.pocketsongs.com

Alto Saxophone

Banjo

Baritone Saxophone

Bassoon

Contents to these albums may be seen on our website at: www.musicminusone.com

Clarinet

Advanced Contest Solos, vol. I	MMO CD 3225
Advanced Contest Solos, vol. II	MMO CD 3226
Advanced Contest Solos, vol. III	MMO CD 3228
Advanced Contest Solos, vol. IV	MMO CD 3229
The Art of the Clarinet: Baermann Method, op. 64 (4 CD Set)	MMO CD 3241
Art Of The Solo Clarinet: Orchestral Excerpts	MMO CD 3206
Band Aids: Concert Band Favorites with Orchestra	MMO CD 3243
BEETHOVEN Quintet for Piano and Winds in E-flat major, op. 16	MMO CD 3235
Beginning Contest Solos, vol. I	MMO CD 3221
Beginning Contest Solos, vol. II	MMO CD 3222
BRAHMS Clarinet Quintet in B minor, op. 115 (Digitally Remastered Version)	MMO CD 3230
BRAHMS Sonata in F minor, op. 120, no. 1; Sonata in E-flat major, op. 120, no. 2	MMO CD 3208
Classic Themes: Student Editions, 27 Easy Songs (2nd-4th year)	MMO CD 3245
Easy Clarinet Solos, vol. I - Student Level	MMO CD 3211
Easy Clarinet Solos, vol. II - Student Level	MMO CD 3212
Easy Jazz Duets for Two Clarinets and Rhythm Section	MMO CD 3213
First Chair Clarinet Solos: Orchestral Excerpts	MMO CD 3205
From Dixie to Swing	MMO CD 3234
HAJDU Jewish Rhapsody for Clarinet, Bass Clarinet and Orchestra	MMO CD 3246
In a League of His Own: Popular Songs played by Ron Odrich and You	MMO CD 3215
Intermediate Contest Solos, vol. I	MMO CD 3223
Intermediate Contest Solos, vol. II	MMO CD 3224
Intermediate Contest Solos, vol. III	MMO CD 3227
Jazz Standards with Rhythm Section (2 CD Set)	MMO CD 3218
Jazz Standards with Strings (2 CD Set)	MMO CD 3219
Jewels for Woodwind Quintet	MMO CD 3232
Masterpieces for Woodwind Quintet	MMO CD 3233
MOZART Clarinet Concerto in A major, KV622 (2 CD Set) includes Bb version	MMO CD 3238
MOZART Quintet for Piano and Winds in E-flat major, KV452	MMO CD 3236
MOZART Quintet in A major, KV581 (2 CD Set) includes Bb version	MMO CD 3207
Popular Concert Favorites with Orchestra	MMO CD 3242
Ron Odrich Plays Standards plus You	MMO CD 3220
SCHUMANN Phantasiestücke, op. 73; 3 Romanzen (3 Romances), op. 94	MMO CD 3210
Sinatra Set to Music: Kern, Weill, Gershwin, Howard and You	MMO CD 3216
SPOHR Clarinet Concerto No. 1 in C minor, op. 26	MMO CD 3203
Stompin' & Struttin' the New Swing: Six Bands on a Hot Tin Roof	MMO CD 3237
STRAVINSKY L'Histoire du Soldat (septet)	MMO CD 3217
Teacher's Partner: Basic Clarinet Studies	MMO CD 3231
The Virtuoso Clarinetist: Baermann Method, op. 63 (4 CD Set)	MMO CD 3240
Visions: The Clarinet Artistry of Ron Odrich (2CD Set)	MMO CD 3214
WEBER Clarinet Concertino, op. 26, J109; BEETHOVEN Piano Trio No. 4, 'Street Song,' op. 11	MMO CD 3204
WEBER Clarinet Concerto No. 1 in F minor, op. 73; STAMITZ Clarinet Concerto No. 3 in B-flat major	MMO CD 3202
WEBER Grand Duo Concertant; WAGNER Adagio	MMO CD 3209
World Favorites: Student Editions, 41 Easy Selections (1st-3rd year)	MMO CD 3244

Double Bass

2+2=5: A Study in Odd Times	MMO CD 2047
The Beat Goes On: Jazz - Funk, Latin, Pop-Rock	MMO CD 4304
Beginning to Intermediate Contest Solos	MMO CD 4301
BOTTESINI Concerto in B minor for Double Bass & Orchestra; Grande Allegro di Concerto for Double Bass & Orchestra	MMO CD 4308
For Bassists Only: Jazz Trios, Quartets, Quintets (Ken Smith)	MMO CD 4303
From Dixie to Swing	MMO CD 4305
Intermediate to Advanced Contest Solos	MMO CD 4302
SCHUBERT Piano Quintet in A major, op. 114, D667 'Forellen-Quintett' or 'Trout Quintet'	MMO CD 4307
STRAVINSKY L'Histoire du Soldat (septet)	MMO CD 4306

Drums

Equipment

See back cover for details

Flute

All MMO albums shown here, may be viewed for their contents at: www.musicminusone.com

French Horn

Visit our two websites: www.musicminusone.com and www.pocketsongs.com

Guitar

Harp

Instructional - Music & Musicians

Oboe

Piano

Piano - continued

RIMSKY-KORSAKOV Piano Concerto in C-sharp minor, op. 30; ARENSKY Fantasia on Russian Folksongs, op. 48....................................MMO CD 3086
RUBINSTEIN Piano Concerto No. 4 in D minor, op. 70....................MMO CD 3079
SCHUBERT Fantasie in F minor, op. 103, D940; Grand Sonata in B-flat major, op. 30, D617 ..MMO CD 3047
SCHUBERT Piano Quintet in A major, op. 114, D667 'Forellen-Quintett' or 'Trout Quintet' ....MMO CD 3087
SCHUBERT Piano Trio in B-flat major, op. 99 (2 CD Set)......................MMO CD 3066
SCHUBERT Piano Trio in E-flat major, op. 100 (2 CD Set)....................MMO CD 3067
SCHUMANN Piano Concerto in A minor, op. 54 ....MMO CD 3008
SCHUMANN Piano Trio in D minor, op. 63 ..MMO CD 3064
SCHUMANN Six Impromptus ('Bilder aus Osten'/ 'Pictures from the East'), op. 66; Children's Ball, op. 130....................MMO CD 3031
Sinatra Standards for Piano and Orchestra: Arranged by Jim Odrich....................MMO CD 3069
STRETCHIN' OUT: 'Comping' with a Jazz Rhythm Section ....MMO CD 3060
TCHAIKOVSKY Fifty Russian Folk Songs ....MMO CD 3042
TCHAIKOVSKY Piano Concerto No. 1 in B-flat minor, op. 23 ....MMO CD 3026
Themes from Great Piano Concerti....................MMO CD 3025
Twenty Dixieland Classics ....MMO CD 3051
Twenty Rhythm Backgrounds to Standards ....MMO CD 3052

Recorder (alto or soprano)

Echoes of Time (2 CD SET) ....MMO CD 3357

Recorder (alto)

Eighteenth Century Recorder Music (2 CD SET) ....MMO CD 3358
Three Sonatas for Alto Recorder, Harpsichord & Viola da gamba (Telemann & Handel)............MMO CD 3341
You Can Play The Recorder: Beginning Adult Method ....MMO CD 3339

Recorder (soprano)

English Consort Music (2 CD SET)................MMO CD 3359
Let's Play The Recorder: Beginning Children's Method ....MMO CD 3338
Playing The Recorder: Folk Songs of Many Nations ....MMO CD 3337
Renaissance Dances and Fantasias ....MMO CD 3356

Recorder (soprano, alto, tenor, or bass)

Dances of Three Centuries ....MMOCD 3360

Soprano Saxophone

Music for Saxophone Quartet ....MMO CD 4801
Stompin' & Struttin' the New Swing: Six Bands on a Hot Tin Roof ....MMO CD 4802

Tenor Saxophone

Band Aids: Concert Band Favorites with Orchestra ....MMO CD 4213
Bluesaxe: Blues for Saxophone, trumpet or clarinet....................MMO CD 4205
Cool Jazz (Rich Maraday)....................MMO CD 4216
Days of Wine & Roses: Sax Section Minus You....................MMO CD 4210
Easy Jazz Duets for Two Tenor Saxophones and Rhythm Section....................MMO CD 4203
Easy Tenor Saxophone Solos: Student Edition, volume 1 ....MMO CD 4201
Easy Tenor Saxophone Solos: Student Edition, volume 2 ....MMO CD 4202
For Saxes Only: Arranged by Bob Wilber, for alto, tenor, baritone sax, trumpet or clarinet....................MMO CD 4204
JOBIM Brazilian Bossa Novas with Strings ....MMO CD 4206
Music for Saxophone Quartet ....MMO CD 4211
Play Lead in a Sax Section ....MMO CD 4209
Popular Concert Favorites with Orchestra ....MMO CD 4212
Sinatra, Sax and Swing (Brian Hayes) ....MMO CD 4217
Stompin' & Struttin' the New Swing: Six Bands on a Hot Tin Roof ....MMO CD 4215
Tenor Jazz Jam (2 CD Set) ....MMO CD 4214
Twenty Dixieland Classics ....MMO CD 4207
Twenty Rhythm Backgrounds to Standards ....MMO CD 4208

Trombone

Advanced Contest Solos, vol. I ....MMO CD 3915
Advanced Contest Solos, vol. II ....MMO CD 3916
Advanced Contest Solos, vol. III ....MMO CD 3917
Advanced Contest Solos, vol. III ....MMO CD 3918
Advanced Contest Solos, vol. V ....MMO CD 3919
Band Aids: Concert Band Favorites ....MMO CD 3930
Baroque Brass and Beyond: Brass Quintets ..MMO CD 3904
Beginning Contest Solos, vol. I ....MMO CD 3911
Beginning Contest Solos, vol. II....................MMO CD 3912
Big Band Ballads for Tenor or Bass Trombone ....MMO CD 3907
Classic Themes: Student Editions, 27 Easy Songs (2nd-3rd year) ....MMO CD 3932
Classical Trombone Solos (2 CD Set) ....MMO CD 3909
Easy Jazz Duets for Two Trombones and Rhythm Section....................MMO CD 3903
Easy Trombone Solos: Student Level, vol, I....MMO CD 3901
Easy Trombone Solos: Student Level, vol, II ..MMO CD 3902
For Trombones Only: More Brass Quintets ..MMO CD 3928
From Dixie to Swing....................MMO CD 3926
Intermediate Contest Solos, vol. I ....MMO CD 3913
Intermediate Contest Solos, vol. II ....MMO CD 3914
Jazz Standards with Strings (2 CD Set) ....MMO CD 3910
Music for Brass Ensemble ....MMO CD 3905
Popular Concert Favorites with Orchestra ....MMO CD 3929
Sticks & Bones Brass Quintets....................MMO CD 3927
STRAVINSKY L'Histoire du Soldat (septet)......MMO CD 3908
Teacher's Partner: Basic Studies, first year ....MMO CD 3920
Twenty Dixieland Classics ....MMO CD 3924
Twenty Rhythm Backgrounds to Standards ....MMO CD 3925
Unsung Hero: Great Sinatra Standards ....MMO CD 3906
World Favorites: Student Editions, 41 Easy Selections (1st-2nd year)....................MMO CD 3931

Trumpet

Tuba/Bass Trombone

Vibes

Viola

Violin

MOZART Violin Concerto No. 1 in B-flat major, KV207;
Rondo Concertant in B-flat major, KV269 ......MMO CD 3161
MOZART Violin Concerto No. 3
in G major, KV216 ....MMO CD 3160
MOZART Violin Concerto No. 4 in D major, KV218;
VIVALDI Concerto in A minor, op.3 no.6........MMO CD 3111
MOZART Violin Concerto No. 5
in A major, KV219 ....MMO CD 3112
Orchestral Favorites, vol. I (Easy Level)..........MMO CD 3122
Orchestral Favorites, vol. II (Med. Level) ......MMO CD 3123
Orchestral Favorites, volume III
(Medium-Difficult Level) ....MMO CD 3124
PROKOFIEV Violin Concerto No. 1 in D major,
op. 19 (1915-1917) ....MMO CD 3178
RAVEL Piano Trio in A minor ....MMO CD 3147
SAINT-SAENS Introduction & Rondo Capriccioso
for Violin & Orchestra; MOZART Serenade No. 5, K204;
Adagio, KV261 ....MMO CD 3116
SCHUBERT Piano Quintet in A major, op. 114, D667
'Forellen-Quintett' or 'Trout Quintet' ....MMO CD 3169
SCHUBERT Piano Trio in B-flat major,
op. 99 (2 CD Set) ....MMO CD 3154
SCHUBERT Piano Trio in E-flat major,
op. 100 (2 CD Set) ....MMO CD 3155
SCHUBERT Three Sonatinas
(Robert Zubrycki, soloist) ....MMO CD 3130
SCHUMANN Piano Trio in D minor, op. 63 ..MMO CD 3152
SIBELIUS Violin Concerto in D minor, op. 47 MMO CD 3144
STRAVINSKY L'Histoire du Soldat (septet)......MMO CD 3146
TCHAIKOVSKY Violin Concerto
in D major, op. 35 ....MMO CD 3102
Teacher's Partner: Basic Violin Studies,
first year...MMO CD 3142
Themes from the major Violin Concerti ....MMO CD 3145
The Three Bs: Bach/Beethoven/Brahms
for Violin & Orchestra ....MMO CD 3125
VIOTTI Violin Concerto No. 22 in A minor ....MMO CD 3114
VIVALDI 'Le Quattre Stagioni' ('The Four Seasons')
for violin and orchestra, op. 8,
nos. 1-4 (2 CD Set) ....MMO CD 3127
VIVALDI 'L'Estro Armonico': Violin Concerti in A minor,
op. 3, no. 6, RV356; Concerto Grosso in A minor,
op. 3, no. 8, RV522; Concerto in D major
op. 3, no.9, RV230 ....MMO CD 3126
VIVALDI Violin Concerto in E major, op. 3, no. 12, RV265;
Violin Concerto in C major, op. 8,
no.6, RV180 'Il Piacere' ....MMO CD 3129
VIVALDI Violin Concerto in E-flat major, 'La Tempesta di
Mare' op. 8, no. 5, RV236; ALBINONI Violin
Concerto in A major.................................MMO CD 3128
WIENIAWSKI Violin Concerto No. 2 in D minor, op. 22;
SARASATE Zigeunerweisen ('Gypsy Ways'),
op. 20 ....MMO CD 3113

Violoncello

C.P.E. BACH Violoncello Concerto
in A minor, Wq170/H432..............................MMO CD 3702
BEETHOVEN Piano Trio No. 8 in E-flat major, WoO38
& Trio No. 11 in G major ('Kakadu' Variations),
op. 121a ....MMO CD 3710
BEETHOVEN String Quartet in A minor,
op. 132 (2 CD Set) ....MMO CD 3713
BEETHOVEN Violoncello Sonata in A major, op. 69;
TELEMANN Violoncello Duet in B-flat............MMO CD 3715
BOCCHERINI Violoncello Concerto in B-flat;
BRUCH Kol Nidrei ....MMO CD 3703

BOLLING Suite For Violoncello
and Jazz Piano Trio ....MMO CD 3706
BRAHMS Double Concerto for Violoncello
& Violin in A minor, op. 102 ....MMO CD 3722
DVORAK Quintet in A major, op. 81 ....MMO CD 3714
DVORAK Violoncello Concerto in B minor,
op. 104 (2 CD Set) ....MMO CD 3701
ELGAR Violoncello Concerto
in E minor, op. 85 ....MMO CD 3720
Great Scott! Ragtime Minus You ....MMO CD 3708
HAYDN Piano Trios, vol. II: G major (HobXV:25),
F-sharp minor (HobXV:26), and F major
(HobXV:6) minus Violoncello ....MMO CD 3717
HAYDN Violoncello Concerto
in C major, HobVIIb:1 ....MMO CD 3718
HAYDN Violoncello Concerto
in D major, HobVIIb:2 ....MMO CD 3719
RAVEL Piano Trio in A minor ....MMO CD 3707
SCHUBERT Piano Quintet in A major, op. 114, D667
'Forellen-Quintett' or 'Trout Quintet' ....MMO CD 3721
SCHUBERT Piano Trio in B-flat major,
op. 99 (2 CD Set) ....MMO CD 3711
SCHUBERT Piano Trio in E-flat major,
op. 100 (2 CD Set) ....MMO CD 3712
SCHUMANN Concerto for Violoncello and Orchestra
in A minor, op. 129; Romantic Concertpieces for 'Cello
and Piano ....MMO CD 3705
SCHUMANN Piano Trio
in D minor, op. 63 ....MMO CD 3709
Ten Concert Pieces for Violoncello
and Piano ....MMO CD 3704
The Cello Soloist: Classic Solos for Cello
and Piano ....MMO CD 3726
WINER Violoncello Concerto; SCHUBERT Ave Maria;
SAINT-SAENS Allegro Appassionato ....MMO CD 3716

Vocal

LEHAR Highlights from Die Lustige Witwe
(The Merry Widow) ....MMO CD 4074
Ten More Classic Vocal Standards ....MMO CD 4051
Twelve Classic Vocal Standards ....MMO CD 4050

Vocal Alto

Oratorio Arias For Alto ....MMO CD 4031

Vocal Bass-Baritone

17th/18th Century Italian Songs - Low Voice,
Volume 1 ....MMO CD 4012
17th/18th Century Italian Songs - Low Voice,
Volume 2 ....MMO CD 4014
Bass-Baritone Arias with Orchestra, vol. I ..MMO CDG 4056
Bass-Baritone Arias with Orchestra, vol. II..MMO CDG 4066
BRAHMS German Lieder - Low Voice ....MMO CD 4006
Everybody's Favorite Songs - Low Voice,
Volume 1 ....MMO CDG 4008
Everybody's Favorite Songs - Low Voice,
Volume 2 ....MMO CDG 4010
Famous Baritone Arias ....MMO CDG 4018
Famous Bass Arias..MMO CDG 4019
Italian Opera Arias for Bass-Baritone
and Orchestra ....MMO CDG 4071
Oratorio Arias For Bass ....MMO CD 4033
SCHUBERT German Lieder - Low Voice,
Volume 2 ....MMO CDG 4004
SCHUMANN German Lieder For Low Voice ..MMO CD 4025
STRAUSS German Lieder For Low Voice ....MMO CD 4023
VERDI Bass-Baritone Arias with Orchestra ....MMO CD 4078
WOLF German Lieder For Low Voice ....MMO CD 4021

Vocal Contralto

Beginning Contralto Solos............................MMO CD 4046

Vocal Mezzo-Soprano

Famous Mezzo-Soprano Arias.......................MMO CDG 4016
French & Italian Opera Arias for Mezzo-Soprano
and Orchestra ....MMO CDG 4062
French Mezzo-Soprano Arias
with Orchestra ....MMO CDG 4086
VERDI Arias for Mezzo-Soprano
with Orchestra ....MMO CDG 4055

Vocal Soprano

17th/18th Century Italian Songs
High Voice, Volume 1 ....MMO CD 4011
17th/18th Century Italian Songs
High Voice, Volume 2 ....MMO CD 4013
Advanced Mezzo Soprano Solos ....MMO CD 4045
Beginning Mezzo Soprano Solos ....MMO CD 4043
Beginning Soprano Solos ....MMO CD 4041
BELLINI La Sonnambula: Scenes and Arias
for Soprano and Orchestra ....MMO CDG 4064
BELLINI Opera Scenes and Arias
for Soprano and Orchestra ....MMO CDG 4063
BRAHMS German Lieder - High Voice............MMO CD 4005
DONIZETTI Soprano Arias with Orchestra..MMO CDG 4058
DVORAK and TCHAIKOVSKY
Soprano Arias with Orchestra......................MMO CDG 4076
Everybody's Favorite Songs
High Voice, Volume 1 ....MMO CDG 4007
Everybody's Favorite Songs
High Voice, Volume 2 ....MMO CDG 4009
Famous Soprano Arias...................................MMO CDG 4015
French Arias For Soprano...............................MMO CD 4029

French Opera Arias for Soprano
and Orchestra ....MMO CDG 4070
Intermediate Mezzo Soprano Solos ....MMO CD 4044
Intermediate Soprano Solos..........................MMO CD 4042
Italian Arias For Soprano ....MMO CD 4028
MOZART Arias For Soprano ....MMO CDG 4026
MOZART Opera Arias for Soprano
and Orchestra, vol. I ....MMO CDG 4060
MOZART Opera Arias for Soprano
and Orchestra, vol. II ....MMO DG 4065
MOZART Opera Arias for Soprano
and Orchestra, vol. III..................................MMO CDG 4087
Oratorio Arias For Soprano ....MMO CD 4030
PUCCINI Arias for Soprano
and Orchestra, vol. II ....MMO CDG 4079
PUCCINI Arias for Soprano
with Orchestra, vol. I ....MMO CDG 4053
SCHUBERT German Lieder
High Voice, Volume 1 ....MMO CDG 4001
SCHUBERT German Lieder
High Voice, Volume 2 ....MMO CDG 4003
SCHUBERT German Lieder
Low Voice, Volume 1 ....MMO CDG 4002
SCHUMANN German Lieder For High Voice..MMO CD 4024
Soprano Arias with Orchestra, vol. I............MMO CDG 4052
Soprano Arias with Orchestra, vol. II ....MMO CDG 4054
STRAUSS German Lieder For High Voice ......MMO CD 4022
VERDI Arias For Soprano ....MMO CDG 4027
VERDI Soprano Arias
with Orchestra, vol. I ....MMO CDG 4059
VERDI Soprano Arias
with Orchestra, vol. II..................................MMO CDG 4072
WOLF German Lieder For High Voice ....MMO CD 4020

Vocal Tenor

Advanced Tenor Solos ....MMO CD 4049
Arias for Tenor and Orchestra
from the repertoire of Andrea Bocelli..........MMO CDG 4069
Beginning Tenor Solos ....MMO CD 4047
Famous Tenor Arias......................................MMO CDG 4017
Intermediate Tenor Solos..............................MMO CD 4048
Italian Tenor Arias with Orchestra ....MMO CDG 4057
Oratorio Arias For Tenor ....MMO CD 4032
PUCCINI Arias for Tenor
and Orchestra, vol. I ....MMO CDG 4061
Romantic Arias for Tenor & Orchestra ....MMO CDG 4085
VERDI Opera Arias for Tenor
and Orchestra ....MMO CDG 4067

F = *Film* • PSCDG: *with Vocals* • JTG: *Just Tracks, Backgrounds only, no vocal*
ST: *Screen Tracks* • PSCD: *with vocals, no graphics*

Visit our two websites: www.musicminusone.com and www.pocketsongs.com